WHAT IS I

(THE ELEMENTS OF PRAYER)

APOSTLE EMMANUEL ADJEI

WHAT IS PRAYER

(The Elements of Prayer)

Apostle Emmanuel Adjei

ISBN: 9798356977671

Write to:

Apostle Emmanuel A. Adjei

fofo275@hotmail.com

INTRODUCTION

The subject of prayer is so huge that we cannot write everything about it in a single book. The interest of this book is to define prayer and to explain what prayer actually means.

This book is not concerned with how to pray or what makes one's prayer get answered or how God answers prayers, even though these are very important questions, but this book has been written to give the reader a clear understanding of what prayer actually is. The purpose of this book is to help you understand, through the scriptures, what we are doing when we pray.

Prayer is the most important thing for a Christian but it is also a subject that many Christians assume they understand and so many feel that they don't need to find out what it actually means to pray. This attitude has become awakens of some Christians.

One cannot deal with any spirit being without prayer. The Jews pray three times a day, the Muslims pray five times a day, the Hindus pray three times a day and the Buddhists pray three times a day. They are all dealing with spirit beings and they pray to these spirit beings, irrespective of what they call them or believe them to be.

Therefore, prayer is a key in the spiritual realm with direct implications in the physical world.

For us Christians we have been commanded to pray without ceasing, not only without ceasing but that everything we do should be done by prayer.

Prayer is therefore a daily necessity if we are going to deal with God.

It is extremely important that we understand prayer. We must know what prayer is. Without prayer, a Christian cannot achieve much, and many of the promises of God or the things God wants for us (or we want God to assist us in getting) will not manifest.

Many people define prayer as 'talking to God and God talking back to you', which is okay but not entirely true and when we define prayer as such, we limit prayer. Because of this, our understanding of what prayer is and what it means to pray is shallow and many Christians are not able to pray. If it is only talking to God then within five minutes we would be done and there will be no need to pray any longer than that.

The reason why it is so important that we define what prayer is so that you can understand it and be able to pray with understanding.

Without understanding of what prayer actually is, you can easily stop praying or you could even stop those prayer habits that are effective and fruitful because you may be deceived into thinking that they do not work.

But before we define prayer, I want us to read a few basic scriptures about praying so that we will know that a Christian can do nothing without prayer that we have been commanded to pray and also that prayer is not an option or a choice but a daily necessity.

BASIC SCRIPTURES ABOUT PRAYING

The scripture says in Philippians that in everything by prayer and supplication we should make known our requests to God, note the statement 'in everything by prayer'. If you are to obey this, it means that you'll be praying almost every day because you will have to pray about everything you will be doing on that day.

Every day, every week and every season you are doing something and so therefore if you are to pray about everything you do, you will be praying daily.

This scripture simply commands us to pray first and foremost about everything we do. Everything by prayer means everything by prayer. It means that if you wake up in the morning, you have to pray, because in the morning you will do something. Even eating is something. Your concerns, your plans and your activities for the day are all things you have to do by prayer.

Be careful for nothing; but in everything by prayer and supplication with thanksgiving let your requests be made known unto God.

Philippians 4:6

The scripture also says in *1 Timothy*, that first of all, prayers must be made for all men. So the first thing that we must do is pray. Supplication, which means asking God with humility and intercession, which means to pray for, are all forms of prayer. Dear reader first means first and therefore the first thing that must be done regarding any situation or circumstance must be prayer.

I exhort therefore, that, first of all, supplications, prayers, intercessions, and giving of thanks, be made for all men

1 Timothy 2:1

In Luke Chapter 18, Jesus taught a whole parable just to show us how we must always pray and not become tired of praying. This shows us how important prayer is and how important the issue of prayer is.

The reason why he spoke the parable is to teach us that we must pray and not get tired. In other words, we have to pray and never give up because you can get tired of praying in general or praying about the same thing over and over again. Never to give up praying is so important that the Lord had to bring a whole set of teachings just to make us understand that prayer is ongoing and that we cannot stop praying, for as Christians, we are simply not allowed to.

Then Jesus told his disciples a parable to show them that they should always pray and not give up.

Luke 18:1

I say that we are not allowed to stop praying as Christians because we have been commanded by the scriptures, in 1 Thessalonians, not to stop praying.

Pray continually.

1 Thessalonians 5:17

Pray continually means to pray always, which implies that we do not stop praying, or is translated as, to pray without ceasing.

We looked at all these scriptures to show us that prayer is a daily necessity and this is from God by God. The Bible never told us whether we should pray seven times or eight times or six times a day.

The rule when it comes to prayer is ***everything by*** *prayer, whilst* you ***pray continually*** and never ***faint***.

Therefore, whether you spend 1 hour praying about everything daily or 15 minutes, the most important thing is that you pray about everything, that your prayers are continuous and that you never get tired of praying. If this means praying two hours straight or 20 minutes morning and evening, it does not matter.

One can't do without prayer when you are going to deal with God. When you are dealing with God as a Christian and you don't pray, you lose out because other people are praying and they are praying for something, probably that same thing that you want!

Others are interacting with spirit beings to help them get whatever result they are seeking, so without asking for God's intervention on our behalf, through prayer, we will be at a huge disadvantage.

Throughout the bible you will see people who were saved only because they prayed or only when prayers were made for them. Below are only three scriptures out of the many for you to read…

Then Isaiah the son of Amoz sent to Hezekiah, saying, "Thus says the LORD God of Israel: 'Because you have prayed to Me against Sennacherib king of Assyria, I have heard.'

2 Kings 19:20

Peter was therefore kept in prison, but constant prayer was offered to God for him by the church. [6] And when Herod was about to bring him out, that night Peter was sleeping, bound with two chains between two soldiers; and the guards before the door were keeping the prison. [7] Now behold, an angel of the Lord stood

by him, and a light shone in the prison; and he struck Peter on the side and raised him up, saying, "Arise quickly!" And his chains fell off his hands.

Acts 12:5-7

because your heart was tender, and you humbled yourself before the LORD when you heard what I spoke against this place and against its inhabitants, that they would become a desolation and a curse, and you tore your clothes and wept before Me, I also have heard you," says the LORD. "Surely, therefore, I will gather you to your fathers, and you shall be gathered to your grave in peace; and your eyes shall not see all the calamity which I will bring on this place." ' " So they brought back word to the king.

2 Kings 22:19-20

WHAT IS PRAYER?

Prayer is when you thank God or petition God or wrestle with God or with spirits or situations, or call forth or push back things or declare or refute or deploy your spiritual weapons for or against, on behalf of a person or yourself or the church or an institution, as you exercise your faith and your spirit man, uttering mysteries in the name of Jesus before God.

I know the definition reads long but prayer is not a simply something that can be defined with just a sentence, as in the case of love. Love cannot be defined with just a sentence, for there are many elements which make up love, so the Bible defines love as kind, patient, as forgiving easily not keeping a record of wrongs…etc, because love involves many things. Thus it is with prayer.

Love is patient, love is kind. It does not envy, it does not boast, it is not proud. It does not dishonor others, it is not self-seeking, it is not easily angered, it keeps no record of

wrongs. Love does not delight in evil but rejoices with the truth. It always protects, always trusts, always hopes, always perseveres.

1 Corinthians 13:4-7

It is important that you really grasp this definition, other than that, you cannot pray without ceasing and you cannot strategically pray. The more you understand prayer, the more you are able to pray. If you don't have a deep understanding of what prayer is, you will stop praying or you will take it for granted. I know it's a long one, but we will now break it down and we will look at each element in detail.

From the above definition, whenever you pray or whenever you seek to pray, you are actually intending to do or you are doing all or some of the elements above, whether you are aware of it or not. By the definition, whenever you pray, you are either ***thanking God or asking God, or wrestling with God or spirit beings or situations, or you are calling into being or pushing out, or you are declaring or refuting, at the same time as deploying your spiritual weapons on behalf or against, either for yourself, for the church, for an institution or for a person, whilst exercising your***

faith and your spirit man, uttering mysteries in the name of Jesus before God.

This is what it means when we pray in Christianity. For example, the Buddhist and Muslims pray differently; their prayers are not even in the name of Jesus.

I would now like to breakdown the definition of prayer step by step, through the scriptures so that we may get a deeper understanding and grasp of prayer.

PRAYER IS THANKING GOD
(Element 1)

When we pray, we are thanking God, because you cannot pray without thanking God. Everybody who prays starts by thanking God, our father in heaven. Prayer involves thanksgiving to God and it is the ignition.

In *Philippians 4*, the scripture was talking about prayer and it told us that in everything by prayer and supplication with thanksgiving we should present our request to God. It teaches us that if we are going to ask God anything, either by prayer or supplication, we are to ask with thanksgiving.

So as you are going to pray to God, you must start with thanksgiving. You cannot approach God in prayer without thanksgiving.

Be anxious for nothing, but in everything by prayer and supplication, with thanksgiving, let your requests be made known to God;

Philippians 4:6

Psalm 100:4 says that we should enter the gates of God with thanksgiving, meaning that first and foremost, we must go before God with thanksgiving. We enter prayer with thanksgiving.

Enter into His gates with thanksgiving, And into His courts with praise. Be thankful to Him, and bless His name.

Psalm 100:4

You will notice thatin*1 Thessalonians* the apostle Paul said that he gives thanks to God always for them, making mention of them in his prayers, meaning that when he is praying he always (please note the word always) thanks God in connection to them in prayer.

We give thanks to God always for you all, making mention of you in our prayers.

1 Thessalonians 1:2

This was also echoed in *Ephesians 1:16* where we are told that he has not stopped giving thanks for them in his prayers. Once again you can see that the thanksgiving in connection to them was in prayer.
So, prayer starts with thanksgiving. To enter into the spirit realm, God expects this.

Therefore I also, after I heard of your faith in the Lord Jesus and your love for all the saints, do not cease to give thanks for you, making mention of you in my prayers:

Ephesians 1:15-16

Jesus always began praying by thanking God. He always offered thanksgiving with words first when he prayed.

Then they took away the stone from the place where the dead man was lying. And Jesus lifted up His eyes and said, "Father, I thank You that You have heard Me.

John 11:41

When you pray and you thank God, you are communicating a message of gratitude towards God…

PRAYER IS ASKING GOD (Element 2)

When you pray you ask God. God is the only person you ask from– Jesus said 'whatever you ask my father'! The type of asking you do in prayer towards God is called petition or supplication, which means not just asking casually but asking for something earnestly or in humility. Therefore, when you pray you're asking God for something with humility and earnestness. You cannot ask God in prayer from the perspective that you are entitled to it or that it is your right or that God owes you, even if what you are asking for has been promised to you by God. Many confuse this with boldness. Boldness however, is confidence that God will hear and answer you.

Be anxious for nothing, but in everything by prayer and supplication, with thanksgiving, let your requests be made known to God;

Philippians 4:6

praying always with all prayer and supplication in the Spirit, being watchful to this end with all perseverance and supplication for all the saints—

Ephesians 6:18

These all continued with one accord in prayer and supplication, with the women and Mary the mother of Jesus, and with His brothers

Acts 1:14

From the three scriptures above you will notice that supplication is attached to prayer, the reason being that supplication is a specific element of prayer where you ask God earnestly in humility. The first scripture says everything by prayer and supplication, the second one says praying always with all supplication and the final one say sin prayer and supplication– and you can see that all are connected and carry the same weight, because supplication is one of the elements of prayer. Please note that supplication is the asking realm of prayer– where we ask God.

You cannot command God; you cannot declare to God, you can only ask Him in humility and earnestness. You cannot bind God and you cannot give Him an ultimatum. That's what the supplication part of prayer means.

The supplication (asking) element of prayer is extreme important because the rule that governs the world or when you're dealing with God, is ask and it shall be given and anyone who asks shall receive.

Ask, and it will be given to you; seek, and you will find; knock, and it will be opened to you. For everyone who asks receives, and he who seeks finds, and to him who knocks it will be opened.

Matthew 7:7-8

So if you don't ask, God is not entitled to give you. God will not necessarily give you what you expect or what you desire; only what you ask Him.

Don't say that God knows so He will do it. The scriptures clearly say –everything by supplication.

The rule is ask and it shall be given to you– not expect and it shall be given; not desire and it shall be given. There's no one who asks and does not receive, as the scripture says; so it means that if you do not ask, there's no obligation for you to receive.

The asking element of prayer is so important. Some people pray, they bind everything, but they forget to ask; they will confess healing, but they forget to ask for healing and therefore they fail because they did not first ask God. No matter what you bind, no matter what you revoke or what you confess, if God does not give it the thumbs up, it won't work.

It is whatsoever you ask, that is what the Father will do. It is not whatsoever you expect. It's not whatsoever you even confessor whatever you feel you are entitled to or just the

fact that the scripture says it so you will have it– No. The scripture says those things so that you will know that they are for you to ask the Father for.
It's what so ever you ask. So when we say we are praying, we are thanking God and we are asking (making supplication to) God to do something specific.

And whatsoever you shall ask in my name, that's will I do, that the Father may be glorified in the Son. If you shall ask anything in my name, I will do it.

John 14:13 -14

The scripture says that Jesus offered prayers and supplication with tears. If Jesus' prayer involved supplication, then when we pray we have no choice other than to ask. We are to pray and ask until we receive. We do not stop asking in prayer when we have not received. Note that it is ok to keeping asking for the same thing in prayer until you receive.

who, in the days of His flesh, when He had offered up prayers and supplications, with vehement cries and tears to Him who was able to save Him from death, and was heard because of His godly fear.

Hebrews 5:7

Therefore when we pray, we are thanking God and asking (making supplication to) God.

PRAYER IS WRESTLING WITH GOD OR SPIRITS OR SITUATIONS (Elements 3)

Many people understand the asking element of prayer and they think that is all prayer is.

When we pray, we are not only asking God, we also wrestle with God or with spirit beings or situations.

When you pray you do not only thank God, you do not only ask, but you are also wrestling with God himself or with spirit beings or situations, which can be anything, including yourself and human beings. When you understand this element of prayer that is when you will understand why there is a need to pray longer and to pray without ceasing.

When God answers your prayers by giving you what you ask of Him, sometimes there are spirit beings called powers, principalities, spiritual wickedness, and rulers of the darkness of this world, that prevent and hinder the manifestation of the answered prayer.

So you've asked God and He is giving it, but the answered prayer is not manifesting because of these evil spirit beings, so now you have to wrestle with them in order for your answered prayers to be released and to manifest. You can only wrestle with them through prayer and by praying.

Sometimes it is not even these evil spirit beings that prevent the answered prayers from manifesting – but you yourself.

It is the wrestling element of prayer that brings in the need for a repetition of the prayer point. Note, it is not the repetition of words but the repetition of the prayer point. Each time you repeat that prayer you realise it becomes more intense and you become more furious and even your voice raises up. You begin to bind spirits and revoke curses and enchantments…etc. That is the wrestling part of prayer; you are wrestling with spirit beings and numerous other situations. Each time you ask God for what He has already answered, He sends angel spirits to go and wrestle with these opposing beings on our behalf, for the manifestation of the answered prayer!

Sometimes you ask God and He is willing to give you what you have asked, but He wants to see if you are serious. So you wrestle with God in order for him to release what He has made up his mind to give you.

It is this wrestling element of prayer that brings in the repetition of a prayer point. Note again, not the repetition of words but of the prayer point. Each time you repeat that prayer you realise it becomes more intense and you may even break down in tears. That is the wrestling; you are wrestling with God.

The scripture teaches us on this element of prayer. The Bible says that we do not wrestle against human beings but against spirit beings called powers, principalities, spiritual wickedness and rulers of the darkness in the spirit realm.

For we do not wrestle against flesh and blood, but against principalities, against powers, against the rulers of the darkness of this age, against spiritual hosts of wickedness in the heavenly places.

Ephesians 6:12

In the book of *Daniel*, we read about how this wrestling happens in the realms of the spirit. It says that when Daniel prayed to God, his prayer was answered but he never received the manifestation of his answered prayer until 21 days after his prayers were answered, and whilst Daniel was still praying the same prayer point.

The Bible teaches us that the reason for the delay in the manifestation of his answered prayer and why he had to pray the same prayer point for 21 days before it manifested, was because the angel who was bringing the answered prayer was being withstood by a spirit being called 'the prince of Persia,' who detained him until another angel came and helped him. As Daniel was praying during those 21 days, repeating the same prayer point, he was actually wrestling for his answered prayer to manifest; He had passed the asking stage of prayer and had entered into the wrestling stage of prayer.

Then he said to me, "Do not fear, Daniel, for from the first day that you set your heart to understand, and to humble yourself before your God, your words were heard; and I have come because of your words. But the prince of the kingdom of Persia withstood me twenty-one days; and behold, Michael, one of the chief princes, came to help me, for I had been left alone there with the kings of Persia. Now I have come to make you understand what will happen to your people in the latter days, for the vision refers to many days yet to come."

Daniel 10:12-14

We also read from the scriptures that Jacob asked God to bless him and God would not. He had to wrestle with God all night before God answered his prayer and blessed him. The scripture acknowledged that he struggled – wrestled – with both God and man and overcame.

Then Jacob was left alone; and a Man wrestled with him until the breaking of day Now when He saw that He did

not prevail against him, He touched the socket of his hip; and the socket of Jacob's hip was out of joint as He wrestled with him. And He said, "Let Me go, for the day breaks. But he said, "I will not let You go unless You bless me!"So He said to him, "What is your name?" He said, "Jacob."And He said, "Your name shall no longer be called Jacob, but Israel; for you have struggled with God and with men, and have prevailed."

Genesis 32:24-28

So when we pray, we do not only thank God, we do not only ask God but we also wrestle. Wrestling is an ongoing tactical striving which demands persistence and stamina. You continue prayer until you receive the answered prayer.

Depending on what you are praying for, the wrestling could be with God or evil spirit beings or situations. This is the wrestling element of prayer.

In the book of Isaiah God said that He set watchmen to cry out unto Him and never give Him rest until He establishes Jerusalem. At the same time He said that it is by Himself that he would establish Jerusalem, He was also asking them to pray to Him until He does it. In other words, He was saying that they should wrestle with Him, for Him to answer them by establishing Jerusalem.

I have set watchmen on your walls, O Jerusalem; They shall never hold their peace day or night. You who make mention of the LORD, do not keep silent, And give Him no rest till He establishes And till He makes Jerusalem a praise in the earth.

Isaiah 62:6-7

When you understand this element of prayer, that is when you understand why there's a need to sit down and pray for an hour straight because it is no more only asking, but also wrestling.

In ***Colossians 4:12***.wewere told that Epaphras was always wrestling in prayer for them. What was he always doing? Wrestling in prayer!

Therefore, when you pray you are wrestling as well and it may well even be with yourself, because it could be your flesh that is opposing what you're asking from God or what He has already answered. This is why the ability to cultivate a habit of praying every day, even if it is for 15 minutes, is important as it breaks the flesh.

Epaphras, who is one of you and a servant of Christ Jesus, sends greetings. He is always wrestling in prayer

for you, that you may stand firm in all the will of God, mature and fully assured.

Colossians 4:12

If you are battling with yourself, you must understand this and wrestle with yourself and overcome yourself. As I said, prayer, like love, is not straightforward, but it is very easy to understand it if you want to.

Therefore ***when we pray we thank God, we ask God and we wrestle in prayer.***

PRAYER IS CALLING FORTH OR PUSHING BACK THINGS (Element 4)

When you pray, you also call forth things into being or you push things back. It's also up to you to call forth good things into being and push bad things away and this is done through prayer.

In *James 5*, the scripture says that Elijah was a human just like us but he said that it would not rain and it didn't rain and he said it would rain and it did rain.

James 5 connects to the scripture in*1 kings 17and 18,* when Elijah said that it would rain and nothing happened until he climbed a mountain and sat down and began to pray. Whilst he was praying he sent this servant to go and look if a cloud had appeared. The appearance of the cloud indicated to him the manifestation of the answered prayer – the rain.

The scripture says that each time, the servant would go and return with a report saying, "I don't see any cloud, 'whilst Elijah was still praying for the rain that he said would fall to fall. It was not until Elijah's servant returned for the seventh time that he reported that he had seen a small cloud.

Notice that when the servant said he had seen a cloud like the hand of a man, Elijah responded to this news by asking the servant to go and tell the king to run home because the rain was about to fall. This meant that all along Elijah was calling forth the rain by his prayers; he was bringing forth the rain into manifestation and that is why he kept asking his servant to see if a cloud had appeared. When he saw that the cloud had indeed appeared he knew that he had brought forth the rain into manifestation and therefore gave the instruction to the king to run home, for the rain was about to fall.

Confess your trespasses to one another, and pray for one another, that you may be healed. The effective, fervent prayer of a righteous man avails much. Elijah was a man with a nature like ours, and he prayed earnestly that it would not rain; and it did not rain on the land for three years and six months. And he prayed again, and the heaven gave rain, and the earth produced its fruit.

James 5:16-18

Now Elijah the Tishbite, from Tishbein Gilead, said to Ahab, "As the LORD, the God of Israel, lives, whom I serve, there will be neither dew nor rain in the next few years except at my word."

1 Kings 17:1

And Elijah said to Ahab, "Go, eat and drink, for there is the sound of a heavy rain." So Ahab went off to eat and drink, but Elijah climbed to the top of Carmel, bent down to the ground and put his face between his knees."Go and look toward the sea," he told his servant. And he went up and looked."There is nothing there," he said. Seven times Elijah said, "Go back."The seventh time the servant reported, "A cloud as small as a man's hand is rising from the sea."So Elijah said, "Go and tell Ahab, 'Hitch up your chariot and go down before the rain stops you.'" Meanwhile, the sky grew black with clouds, the wind rose, a heavy rain started falling and Ahab rode off to Jezreel.

1 Kings 18:41-45

The Bible clearly stated that Elijah was a human like me and like you and he said that it wouldn't rain and it didn't and he said that it would rain and it did. The Bible clearly showed us that it was in prayer and through prayer by his word that he determined whether it would rain or not. This is to teach us that we can pull things forth or push them back through prayer.

We need to understand this so that we will understand prayer and enjoy persistent prayer. Sometimes the only reason why a person doesn't get what he or she has asked God for is that they did not pull it through.

By this, God is showing us another side of prayer. He prayed and asked God for it not to rain. He prayed and said that it would not rain based on what he asked God for and it did not rain.

Again he prayed that it would rain and it rained. So the onus was on Him, (in the Lord of course and in the name of Jesus), and not on God to have to do it.

He pulled the rain in by his word, through prayer, and that is where the authority of a Christian comes in Prayer is where the authority you have as a believer is exercised. At your word, in the name of Jesus in prayer, you determine what will come to pass by pulling it forth or out with fervent prayer, as the scripture in *James* tells us. So when we pray to God it is not only asking God but we are also pulling what we want in, based on our authority as believers.

A clear example is when we are dealing with demons, they do not come out of a person because we ask God that the demons should come out; they come out of a person because we, in the name of Jesus, cast them out, as the scripture says!

When we tell demons to come out in the name of Jesus they do, but when don't, they just relax and will stay there because we never commanded them to come out.

PRAYER IS DECLARING OR REFUTING A THING (Element 5)

When we pray we also declare or refute a thing or a cause. *Job 22: 28*said that you shall declare a thing and it shall be established for you. It means that what you declare is what will happen to you. The word 'declare' is an authoritative word. It shows us that you say what you want to see with power not just casually. It is this part of prayer that many call' confessing'– which is speaking out that which you want to see. But effective confessing– speaking out or saying that which you wish to see is done in prayer, through declaration. This means saying it as you want it to happen for you, in the name of Jesus, by the power of the Holy Spirit, in the presence of God.

You will also declare a thing, And it will be established for you; So light will shine on your ways.

Job 22:28

So when you pray, you are not only thanking God, you are not only asking Him, you are not only wrestling, you are not only pulling forth what you're asking for, but you are also declaring what you desire to see by speaking what should happen and how your future should look like. You bring it into being by your words as you declare it. However, this is not done casually– it won't work that way– because your words without God's power carry no power in terms of the demonic or spiritual realms. Further, you do not only declare things, you also refute things. Yes, in prayer you refute as well. The word refute is also authoritative. You refute all your fears, what you do not wish to see come to pass in your life or regarding a particular issue and what people have spoken against you. People are always speaking and desiring evil against others. People make evil predictions against others all the time.

No weapon formed against you shall prosper, And every tongue which rises against you in judgment You shall condemn. This is the heritage of the servants of the LORD, And their righteousness is from Me," says the LORD.

Isaiah 54:17

The above scripture says that no weapon formed against you shall prosper. But why won't it prosper? The scripture tells us – because you shall refute it and because this is also your heritage, meaning that you are to cause it not to come to pass by refuting it.

It is in prayer that you refute those things which are spoken against you, for the bible says that our weapons are not carnal but mighty to the pulling down of strongholds. If you fail to refute these things, especially those which were set in motion by people's words, what they have spoken might succeed against you, for the scripture in *proverbs* says that life and death are in the power of the tongue. The power there means that the words have been spoken under an authority.

Death and life are in the power of the tongue, And those who love it will eat its fruit.

Proverbs 18:21

It is therefore in prayer that you refute all words and weapons used against you by saying what will not succeed against you and what you will not see; by rejecting and cancelling those things by your words, through the power of the Holy Spirit, in the name of Jesus Christ. The reason why this is most effective in prayer is that it will be in the presence of God. You must love to declare and refute as you pray, because those who love it will eat of its fruit, as the scripture says. The fruits are the manifestation of whatever is being refuted or declared. You can liken this part of prayer to you holding a letter stamp with sheets of results and the results that you accept or reject are in your hands. The burden to refute or to declare is on you, for the scripture tells us that it is you who shall refute and declare.

Prayer is not only asking, it's not only thanksgiving, it's not only wrestling, it's not only pulling forth, but it's also declaring and refuting.

When I see people who I know don't give attention to prayer, I think what a grave error, because that is how you decide your future. Prayer is a priority; the bible tells us 'everything by prayer'. That is how you decide your future! That's how you map your world for tomorrow!

PRAYER IS DEPLOYING YOUR SPIRITUAL WEAPONS (Elements 6)

When we pray, we also deploy our spiritual weapons. *2 Corinthians10:3-5* is clear about this.

For though we walk in the flesh, we do not war according to the flesh. For the weapons of our warfare are not carnal but mighty in God for pulling down strongholds, casting down arguments and every high thing that exalts itself against the knowledge of God, bringing every thought into captivity to the obedience of Christ.

2 Corinthians 10:3-5

We have weapons in our possessions as Christians and as the scripture says, these weapons are not physical ones. So in other words, these weapons that we have at our possession are spiritual, very mighty and very powerful in pulling down anything. Now, these weapons are deployed in prayer. As you begin to pray, you begin to deploy these weapons without even knowing it. How do we know this? *Ephesians 6* teaches us…

In *Ephesians 6:12-18*, the scripture was talking about the spiritual forces that we wrestle with and it went on to say, that because we are fighting spirit beings who are not flesh, we should put on the full armour of God; prayer was clearly mentioned as an addition to this armour. You will see that all these pieces of armour were protective (for defence), apart from one– the sword – the only piece for offence. This means that as we are fully clothed with this spiritual military gear, ready for warfare, we begin to release and deploy the offensive weapon, that is, the word of God(the sword of the Spirit),which deploys all the weapons of God.

And take the helmet of salvation, and the sword of the Spirit, which is the word of God; praying always with all prayer and supplication in the Spirit, being watchful to this end with all perseverance and supplication for all the saints—

Ephesians 6:17-18

The scripture also said that the Lord answers by fire and also, that only a raging fire will consume the adversaries of the Lord. Meaning that as we pray, fire is also released to consume the enemies of God, who are our enemies as well.

Our prayers release an inferno of fire, which is one of the weapons that is released as you pray.

Then you call on the name of your gods, and I will call on the name of the LORD; and the God who answers by fire, He is God."So all the people answered and said, "It is well spoken."

1 Kings 18:24

But only a fearful expectation of judgment and of raging fire that will consume the enemies of God.

Hebrews 10:27

So once you pray, you begin to deploy spiritual weapons that you don't even know. Yes, believe me, one day I was praying. I was praying and the Lord opened my eyes and I saw that there was something like an automatic machine gun around my waist like a belt and as long as I was praying, the machine gun was firing bullets like fire. I never imagined that such a weapon existed, but I saw it. Several times the Lord has opened my eyes during prayer and I have seen fire or Holy Ghost fire and I will see this fire going on people and onto places.

This is one of the reasons why it is so important to pray in tongues as well.

Therefore, without praying and going beyond the asking realm of prayer, you will not receive much because when we pray, we do not only thank, we do not only ask, we do not only strive and wrestle, nor do we only declare and decree but we also deploy our spiritual weapons.

PRAYER IS DECLARING OF FAITH (Elements 7)

When you pray you also declare or you release your faith. Prayer is an act of faith. When you pray, you are saying that you really believe all that the Bible says about prayer and most importantly, you have faith in God as one who hears and acts when we involve Him by prayer. If you truly believe (have faith) that God hears and answers prayer, you will never stop praying until you get a result.

In *Luke 8* we read that Jesus taught a whole parable to tell us that we must never cease to pray. Jesus used a parable about a woman who persisted in seeking justice from an unjust judge and we learn that the only reason why she received justice from this unjust judge was because of her persistent asking.

Jesus concluded that even if this unjust judge gave the woman justice, how much more will God, who *is* just, answer us if we persist in asking Him. This is assurance to us.

But then one may wonder why God should want us to keep asking Him for the same thing over and over again, before we receive an answer? Jesus gave us the answer in the parable that is – faith –"That God will find faith on earth".

Meaning, that persistent prayer is a demonstration of our faith to God. In other words, God has designed prayer so that we will demonstrate our faith as we continue to ask of Him.

Then Jesus told his disciples a parable to show them that they should always pray and not give up.

Luke 18:1

And the Lord said, "Listen to what the unjust judge says. And will not God bring about justice for his chosen ones, who cry out to him day and night? Will he keep putting them off? I tell you, he will see that they get justice, and quickly. However, when the Son of Man comes, will he find faith on the earth?

Luke 18:6-8

He is the Rock, his works are perfect, and all his ways are just. A faithful God who does no wrong, upright and just is he.

Deuteronomy 32:4

Therefore, when you pray, you are not only asking and deploying your spiritual weapons, but you are also deploying faith. Remember, faith is not what you say but what you do.

PRAYER IS UTTERING MYSTERIES (Element 8)

When we pray, we are to utter mysteries by praying in the Spirit. The Bible clearly commands that we are to pray in words and also with our spirit, which is praying in tongues.

For if I pray in a tongue, my spirit prays, but my mind is unfruitful. So what shall I do? I will pray with my spirit, but I will also pray with my understanding; I will sing with my spirit, but I will also sing with my understanding.

1 Corinthians 14:14-15

The bible says that when you pray in tongues you utter mysteries. When you pray in tongues you ask, declare, refute and say things that there is no way your mind can even imagine or comprehend; and things that you do not even have the vocabulary to speak it out! You mention and say mysterious things as you pray in tongues. Sometimes in your prayers you've asked and said everything, but you'd be surprised that the most important thing to say in your prayer will not even come into mind. But as you pray in tongues, the Spirit helps you and one of the ways He helps you is by giving utterances whilst you speak in tongues…

For anyone who speaks in a tongue does not speak to people but to God. Indeed, no one understands them; they utter mysteries by the Spirit.

1 Corinthians 14:2

In the same way, the Spirit helps us in our weakness. We do not know what we ought to pray for, but the Spirit himself intercedes for us through wordless groans.

Romans 8:26

A true prayer must come with praying in tongues. Praying in tongues is one of the kinds of prayers we should be praying. The Bible clearly tells us that we should pray all kinds of prayer and to pray in the Spirit– which is praying in tongues.

Pray in the Spirit at all times, with every kind of prayer and petition. To this end, stay alert with all perseverance in your prayers for all the saints.

Ephesians 6:18

PRAYER IS BUILDING YOURSELF UP (Element 9)

When you pray, you do not only ask God or demonstrate your faith but you also build up your spirit.

Anyone who speaks in a tongue edifies themselves, but the one who prophesies edifies the church.

1 Corinthians 14:4

But you, beloved, building yourselves up on your most holy faith, praying in the Holy Spirit,

Jude 20

As you pray in tongues in prayer, you edify yourself. The word 'edifies' means you build yourself up. It is in prayer that our spirit senses are sharpened and the Spirit of God is also poured on us, to build us up. Because of this element of prayer, it is important that one spends sometime to pray only in tongues in order to build himself up spiritually. You can never be built up nor be strong spiritually without building up your spirit man. There is a direct relationship between how spiritually effective you are and how well your spirit man has been built up.

I myself have a prayer routine; I start with worshiping God by singing to him, then I thank God, then I ask for the forgiveness of sin and then I wear the full armour of God, as the scripture instructs.

Once I finish the above routine I always pray in the spirit, no words, for a few minutes before I start asking God in prayer. I do this to first utter mysteries and then to build myself up, to help me pray better.

PRAYER IS ASKING AND SPEAKING IN THE NAME OF JESUS (Element 10)

When we pray, our requests and our wrestling, or declarations and our demonstrations of faith, and all the elements of prayer are done in the name of Jesus. The name Jesus gives us the authority to go before God in prayer, to ask Him and also to exercise all the elements of prayer.

You must always declare at the beginning and end of your prayer that it is in the name of Jesus that you are praying and also, that it is in the name of Jesus that you ask and exercise all the elements of prayer. When you pray in the name of Jesus it means that you have not come to God of your own accord or right but in Christ Jesus, whom no sin was found. Without asking in the name of Jesus it is more likely that our prayer is not to God Almighty, because that is the only name that has been given unto men to assess God.

Jesus said in *John 16* that God will give us whatever we ask in His name. So we ask in the name of Jesus. When you remove the part where you ask in the name of Jesus, it is no more a prayer to God Almighty because the scripture is clear that no one comes to God except through Jesus. In the context of prayer it also teaches that the way to God is only through Jesus and therefore, if we are praying to God, the only way to Him is through Jesus – by His name and His authority.

The Hindus pray and the Muslims pray, but their prayers are not to our God. That's why they don't pray in the name of Jesus. We pray to our Father in heaven, in the name of Jesus, which is what makes our prayer to God. Hindu prayers focus on the personal forms of Devas and/or Devis and the Muslim prayers are to Allah in the name of Mohammed, because they pray with Mohammad's name…

In that day you will no longer ask me anything. Very truly I tell you, my Father will give you whatever you ask in my name. Until now you have not asked for anything in my name. Ask and you will receive, and your joy will be complete.

John 16:23-24

Jesus answered, "I am the way and the truth and the life. No one comes to the Father except through me.

John 14:6

PRAYER IS BEING IN THE PRESENCE OF GOD (Element 11)

The final part of our definition is that as you are praying, as you are asking, as you are refuting, as you are declaring and as you are wrestling, you are doing all that in the name of Jesus, before God. You must believe that the moment you say that you are praying in the name of Jesus, you are before the presence of God. You must believe that as you pray you are before God Almighty. I am always mindful that I'm before God when I am praying.

If it is not before God, then where is your prayer going and who are you praying to because God is real! When you are praying know that what makes it prayer is that it is done in the name of Jesus Christ, before God Almighty and that you're not just speaking into the air or the wind.

Hebrews 4 tells us that we should come before God with confidence that we may obtain mercy. You won't see God anywhere you go to physically or at a geographical location and therefore, coming to God means in prayer, and in a Holy convocation. *Psalm 141* says 'let my prayer be set before you as incense'.

Revelation 5:8 shows us that our prayers are in a bowl before God as incense. Therefore, the moment that you pray, your prayer is going before God and so you *must* know and believe that you are before God.

Let us then approach God's throne of grace with confidence, so that we may receive mercy and find grace to help us in our time of need.

Hebrews 4:16

May my prayer be set before you like incense; may the lifting up of my hands be like the evening sacrifice.

Psalm 141:2

And when he had taken it, the four living creatures and the twenty-four elders fell down before the Lamb. Each one had a harp and they were holding golden bowls full of incense, which are the prayers of God's people.

Revelation 5:8

In Prayer you must be aware that you are before God. So when we are praying in church and people are chewing gum, fidgeting or absent-mindedly walking around, showing no reverence or seriousness, it is a major indication that they are not actually aware and don't really believe that they are praying before God. The moment you make up your mind to pray from your heart, you move into another realm; the realm of the presence of God.

May the grace to pray effective prayers come upon you and may you pray more effectively than ever before, in the name of Jesus. Do not forget to ***thank God, petition God, wrestle with God, with spirits or situations, to call forth, push things back or declare, to refute or deploy your spiritual weapons, as you exercise your faith and your spirit man, uttering mysteries in the name of Jesus before God***– now more than ever.

GOD BE WITH YOU

Printed in Great Britain
by Amazon